Whitburn Cricket Club
150 Not Out

A Pictorial History of Whitburn Cricket Club
1862 – 2012

John Yearnshire

Introduction

This history of Whitburn Cricket Club happened by chance. For some time I had been researching the Baronets Williamson, the last owners of the historic Whitburn Hall, when the cricketing prowess and largesse of the 8th Baronet Sir Hedworth Williamson took on a life of its own.

The cricket ground was created through his generosity when he gave part of his garden to be the cricket ground. Later he even captained the club.

Last year I became a committee member of this excellent club. While discussing the programme for 150th anniversary celebrations I realised that production of a historic record would fit into the celebration events. This created some pressure to achieve the deadline as so many interesting people wished to contribute. This is not a definitive history of cricket in Whitburn, it can't be, rather it is mainly a pictorial record of important and interesting milestones. I hope you enjoy the book.

Who knows in 50, 100 or even 150 years into the future members may find this and peer into the past with awe.

John Yearnshire
BA (Hons) M.A. ABIPP

With Best Wishes
John. R. Yearnshire
2015.

In Victorian times cricket was quite well established in the ancient village of Whitburn. It was the custom for the teams to carry round their own sign, and the Whitburn team took their beautifully painted "The Fighting Man" on all their travels. Sadly, there appears to be no existing image of this remarkable regalia; however, they certainly had it in their possession at one of their matches in 1856 at Whickham, near Gateshead, when a hard fought game resulted in a spirited brawl between the players. (Echo. C.A.Smith)

In 1861 Baronet Sir Hedworth Williamson, who had the previous year inherited the title and Whitburn Hall on the death of his father, decided to formalise the honourable game. He appears to have been a larger than life character and a great cricket enthusiast. Historical record shows that he called his butler in to see him and this meeting led to the formation of the present day Whitburn Cricket Club.

In spring of 1862, Sir Hedworth gave permission for part of his garden to be used as a cricket field. This meant that he could look out onto the area of play from the south facing windows of Whitburn Hall. The only downside was that there was a huge sycamore tree twenty two yards onto the new cricket ground and the players had no choice but to 'play around' it. He said no one was to pay a fee to see the games and Sir Hedworth is reputed to have stipulated one condition and that was that balls were not to fall within the lawned area which remained as his garden frontage. Therefore if a batsman smashed a ball and it went outside the playing area, it was to be counted as neither a four nor a six if it landed within the Hall curtilage.

Most of the cricketers in the village joined the club, as well as some of the hall workers. On Whit Monday a match was played between two elevens of the club, who afterwards 'partook of an excellent dinner and spent an agreeable evening' (presumably at the hall).

On Whit Tuesday the first match proper was played between Whitburn and Monkwearmouth Eden which Whitburn won by 35 runs. The totals being Whitburn 105 runs, Monkwearmouth Eden 73 runs.

As the team of diverse people gelled together, and their cricketing competence increased, they became a team to be reckoned with as they 'toured North-East villages through countless summers.' Whitburn won fame for their battling qualities against technically stronger opposition.

Sir Hedworth Williamson appeared in games during the early period of the club's formation as well as being President of the club. We would describe him today as an all rounder and match details of a game played between Whitburn and Sunderland in 1865 show that he scored 13 runs not out and took three wickets (see score card details next page).

The pewter teapot presented in addition to a purse of gold, in 1880 to Mr. John Young in recognition of his services as a bowler to Whitburn Cricket Club.

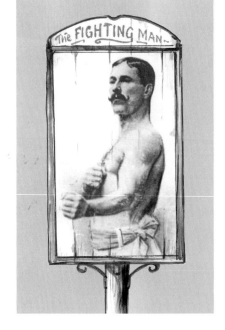

Sir Hedworth was connected with the judiciary and when the courts were sitting during the Durham or Newcastle Assizes he arranged cricket matches between the visiting Judges and lawyers and the Whitburn team.

Artist impression of 'The Fighting Man' sign.

The Whitburn team and details were:

Marton Carr b Hall		19
Charles Carr c Iliff b Hall	...	9
F. Wilcox c Iliff b Stubley	...	1
H. Bell c Stubley b Johnston	...	34
W. Tinkler run out		2
T. Moore c Stubley b Johnston		2
F. Kelsey hit wicket		5
W. Brown b Johnston		5
Sir Hedworth Williamson n.o.	..	13
Spraggon b Johnston		2
Extras (2 byes, 6 leg byes		8
Total		102

The Sunderland side fared as follows :—

W. Stubley run out		24
T. Veitch b Sir Hedworth Williamson		14
J. Peacock c Wilcox b Kelsey		10
S. Hall b Wilcox		17
T. Potts run out		6
G. Pawson b Spraggon		3
E. Iliff b Sir Hedworth Williamson		6
G. Johnston b Spraggon		9
A. Elliott b Spraggon		5
J. Hartley c Kelsey b Sir Hedworth Williamson		6
H. P. Kayll not out		0
Extras (6 wides, 5 byes 1 leg bye)		12
Total		112

Sir Hedworth Williamson 8th Baronet, President and Club Captain.

Sir Hedworth Williamson photographed with both cricketers and officials. During the match between, Whitburn Cricket Club and the Judges and Lawyers team in 1880.

Standing ?, Mr. Little, ?, W.D. Allison, Fritz Williamson, Mr. Tinkler, Mr.Raine, Middle Row Sir Hedworth Williamson, C. Dobson, T.K. Dobson, ?, Mr. Hawley. Front Row W. Hogg, C. Hawley, Cud Hall, ?.

Sir Hedworth Williamson had the honour of becoming the first president of Durham County Cricket Club in 1882 and held this position until 1886.

His son Frederick Charles Williamson played cricket for both Whitburn and in 1899 Durham County Cricket Club.

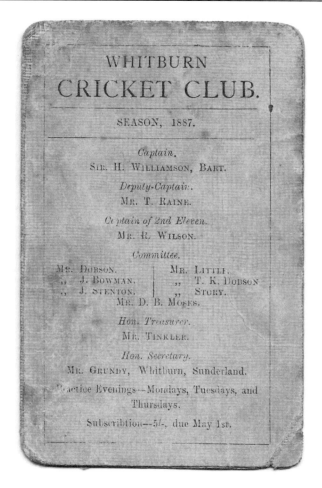

Whitburn cricket fixture booklet and list of officials 1887.

The roller, here being used in the 1950's, was cast at Penshaw Iron Foundry in 1880 at a cost of £22. Sir Hedworth Williamson agreed to pay half of the cost; astonishingly this roller is still in use at the club today.

In 1886, The Sunderland Herald and Post reported on the 29th September, 'That this well known cricket club celebrated the conclusion of its 25th season with nearly 40 members and friends who sat down to dinner served in the Misses Tinkler's (Whitburn) best style. After dinner songs, toasts and recitations helped to pass a very pleasant evening. Cordial votes of thanks were passed to the captain Sir Hedworth Williamson, the vice captain Mr. Raine, the Hon. Secretary Mr A Grundy and to Mr Dobson for presiding'.

From the secretary's report the first team played 19 matches, won 10, drew 6 and lost only 3.

League Champions cap 1896.

*Sir Hedworth Williamson was also the first
President of Durham County Cricket Club
1882-1886.*

*Mr Grundy Hon Secretary
Whitburn Cricket Club.*

Durham County League Championship winners 1896 and 1898 with Sir Hedworth Williamson.

Whitburn Cricket Club Team late 1890's early 1900's pictured in front of the hall gates.

Whitburn Cricket Club team on their travels to Burnmoor shortly before the First World War, sitting front left a very young J.P.T. 'Percy' Bell.

Another early image of Whitburn Cricket Club posed outside the pristine hall gates.
A close look shows the gold painted tops of the gates, unfortunately the gates
are currently in a state of disrepair.

Whitburn First X1 1919
Merriman (umpire) J.P.T. Bell, J. Seed, W. Browning, C. Sweeting, J.R. Taylor, A. Leadbitter,
J. Maddison, Rawlings, Allison (Capt.) T.K. Dobson, J. Shiel
(young scorer).

The official opening of the new pavilion in 1921 by Mr Grundy (centre wearing bowler hat) and J.T. Bell with arm around fence. The pavilion was purchased from Messrs Holloway at a cost of £120.

Seated in front of the new pavilion in1921 Whitburn First X1
K. Oates, ?, W. Nunn, J. Maddison, J. Maddison, J.M. Davison, W. Browning, J.P.T. Bell, ?, J.T. Bell, ?, J. Kellsall, A.P. Ashley, T.K. Dobson, J.W. Smith, C. Sweeting.

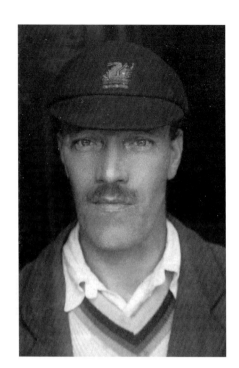

Arthur Percival (AP) Ashley
Whitburn Cricket Club captain and local headmaster.

A.P. Ashley and Adolph Hitler had been at the first day of the battle of Somme in 1916 and both survived. Immediately after the war, Ashley played a match against Whitburn, during which the Rector of Whitburn offered him the headmastership of the village school if he would leave Durham City and come and play for Whitburn Village. That's one way of recruiting talent.

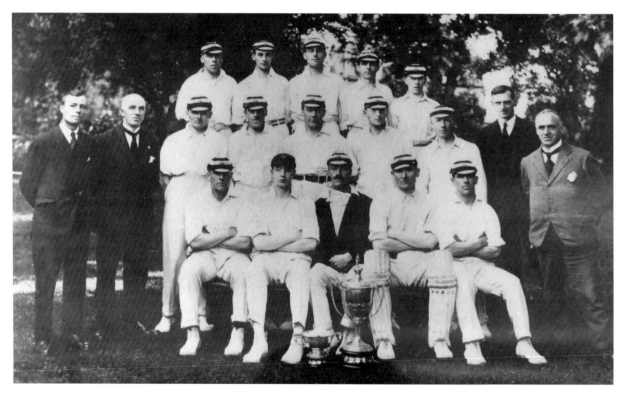

Whitburn Cricket Club
Durham Senior League Champions. 1923 Winners of Saunders Cup. 1921-23.

J.W. Smith, J. Donnan, F. Henderson, C. Sweeting, T. Calvert,
O.F. Barkes, C.J. Oates, R. Percy, J.P.T. Bell, J. Shiel, W.A. Dobson, J. Kelsall, W. Nunn, J.T. Bell,
T.G. Smith, T.K. Dobson, A.P. Ashley (Capt), J. Maddison, W. Browning.

Whitburn produced cricketing dynasties. Two are mentioned here though there will be many more. The Dobson family from Whitburn Village produced six Durham County Cricketers: Thomas Kell Dobson Senior 1886-1896; his three brothers Fred Dobson 1888, Charles Lancelot Dobson 1897-1901 and William Spencer Dobson 1898-1905; Thomas Kell Dobson Junior 1922-1936 his brother William Allison Dobson 1919-1925.

***Thomas Kell Dobson Junior 1901-1940
one of the finest all rounders to represent
Durham County Cricket Club and
Whitburn Cricket Club.***

Thomas Kell Dobson Junior was born in 1901 and described as a splendid all rounder for Whitburn Cricket Club; he represented the Durham County Cricket club from 1922-1936. He also captained the county from 1932-1936.

Thomas was probably the most talented cricketer ever to play for Whitburn and described by Durham County Cricket historian Brian Hunt as one of the finest all-rounders to play for Durham County. He represented Durham in 100 matches and scored 3,040 runs, at an average of 24.51. He also took 226 wickets, at an average of 16.70.

He hit 15 fifties and scored 5 centuries including 105 against the West Indies in 1928.

He took 7 wickets in an innings on three occasions, with his best performance being 7 for 25 against Staffordshire in 1931. He also represented the Minor Counties X1 on several occasions. He resigned the captaincy in 1937 owing to ill health, and died sadly in 1940 aged only 39 years - a great miss to his family and cricket.

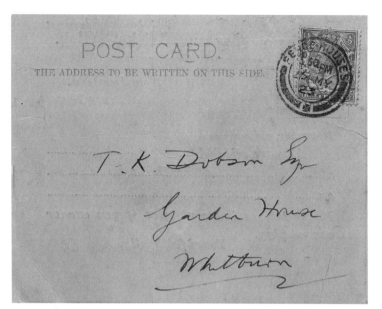

Postcard informing T.K. Dobson of his selection for Durham County Cricket Club in 1923.

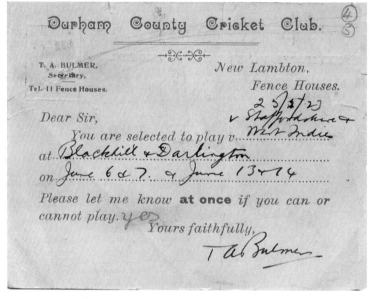

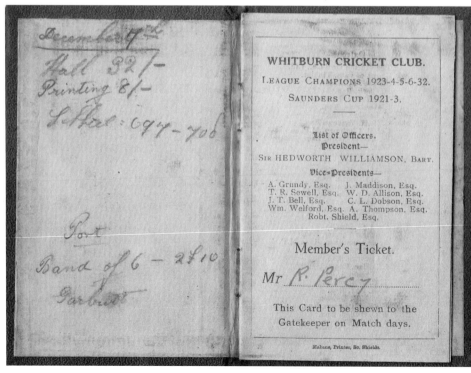

Mr. R.H. Percy's members ticket for the 1934 season.

The following players all played for Whitburn Cricket Club in the 1923 Durham Senior League winning team and all went on to represent Durham County Cricket Club, a very rare achievement from a small village club. During the most successful period of Whitburn Cricket Club they did not have a paid professional in their squad yet won the Durham Senior League five times in nine years.

J.W. Smith

A.P. Ashley

J.P.T. Bell

T.G. Smith

W.A. Dobson

T.K. Dobson Jnr

J. Kelsall

Whitburn Cricket Club's opening batsmen during the successful 1920's period
J.P.T (Percy) Bell and T.K. Dobson, both batsmen represented Durham County Cricket Club.

The Smith Family of Whitburn

L to r Tom Smith, Jim Smith, Billy Smith, Sep Smith, Joseph Smith, Jack Smith.

Whitburn cricketers Billy and Jack Smith were in the Portsmouth side beaten 2-1 by Manchester City in the FA Cup Final at Wembley in 1934 in front of a crowd of 93,258.

Billy and Jack are two of the many members of the Smith family to play for Whitburn over the years. Joe, Jim and Tom (known as Tosser) also played around this time.

Billy's son Eric played for Whitburn through five decades, finally retiring in 1993; his son Michael also played for the village club. Currently, 2 year old grandson George is showing signs of following the family tradition. Eric is a former club president and currently President of the Durham Senior League.

Eric Smith *Sunderland Echo Cartoon 1972.* *Eric's son Michael Smith.*

Whitburn Cricket Club team shortly after the Second World War
A. Alder, R.H. Percy, A. Farrar, R. Paxton, W. Calvert, ?, ?, W. Scott, ?, ?, ?.

Spectators watching a game at Whitburn during the 1950's against local rivals Sunderland. How styles change!

Captain, First Team:
Mr. R. H. Percy.
Vice-Captain, First Team:
Mr. A. M. Farrar.
Captain, Second Team:
Mr. R. Young.
Vice-Captain, Second Team:
Mr. T. Reed.
Captain, Third Team:
Mr. L. P. Young.
Committee:
Messrs. A. Alder, J. B. Bell, J. Hope,
A. McMahon, J. Nunn, R. W. Paxton,
G. Russell, W. Shiel.
Honorary Auditors:
Messrs. A. P. Ashley and F. Raine.
Honorary Secretary:
Mr. T. Calvert,
2 Bowman Street, Whitburn.
Honorary Treasurer:
Mr. J. P. T. Bell,
69 Adolphus Street, Whitburn.
Honorary Assistant Secretary:
Mr. R. Emmerson.
Honorary Assistant Treasurer:
Mr. R. Heron.

FIRST TEAM FIXTURES

Date 1950	Opponents	Ground	Result
April 29	Durham City	away	....
May 6	South Shields	away	....
,, 13	Horden	home	....
,, 20	Boldon	home	....
,, 27	Wearmouth	away	....
,, 29	Eppleton	away	....
June 3	Chester-le-Street	away	....
,, 10	Philadelphia	home	....
,, 17	Seaham Harbour	away	....
,, 24	Sunderland	home	....
July 1	Burnmoor	home	....
,, 8	Durham City	home	....
,, 15	South Shields	home	....
,, 22	Horden	away	....
,, 29	Boldon	away	....
Aug. 5	Wearmouth	home	....
,, 7	Eppleton	home	....
,, 12	Chester-le-Street	home	....
,, 19	Philadelphia	away	....
,, 26	Seaham Harbour	home	....
Sept. 2	Sunderland	away	....
,, 9	Burnmoor	away	....

Whitburn cricket club fixture list and club officials 1950.

Whitburn Cricket Club Cap 1950's.

16

Whitburn Cricket Club First X1
Durham Senior League Champions 1950
A. Alder, A. Farrar, J. Nunn,
J.P.T. Bell, E. Mapstone, R. Heron, K. Kirsten, S. O'Linn, A. Coulthard,
R. Sewell, J. Bell, R. Emmerson, R. Percy, S. Leary, T. Calvert.

'Team of Footballers'
Durham Senior League Champions 1950

Whitburn became league champions in 1950, the previous year having been bottom of the league or 'wooden-spoonist'. This was in some way due to the inclusion of three South Africans - Sid O'Linn, Stuart Leary and Ken Kirsten; they had travelled to England to play football for the then First Division club Charlton Athletic.

Charlton's Blackhill born manager Jimmy Seed, a personal friend of J.P.T. 'Percy' Bell, encouraged them to spend the summer playing cricket for the village side. Leary and O'Linn went on to play professional cricket for Kent and the latter played seven test matches for the 'Springboks.' He also represented South Africa at international football.

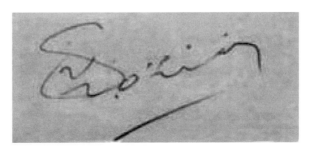

Sid O'Linn's autograph

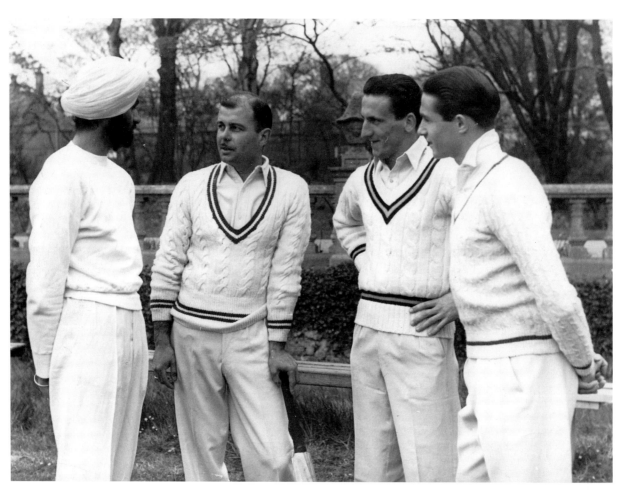

*The three South Africans Ken Kirsten,
Sid O'Linn, Stuart Leary with Singh Dougal
at Whitburn.*

*Jimmy Seed a member of the Whitburn
Cricket team of 1919.
Successful footballer and manager of
Charlton Athletic.*

In 2012 Richard Heron is believed to be the oldest surviving club player at 98 years of age. He has always loved the game of cricket. Whilst reading law at Trinity Hall, Cambridge, he played for the cricket X1 and was vice captain under the captaincy of a gentleman by the name of Donald Duart Mclean, who he described as a normal good guy, someone he got to know very well. "I was quite shocked when I discovered he was a notorious spy." (Burgess/McLean)

Richard Heron played for Whitburn cricket club after short spells with both South Shields and Sunderland. However, when he heard that Whitburn were looking for players he decided to join them.

He describes the 1950's Durham Senior League winning side, as having no individual stars, but rather one all round team where they all worked for each other.

In the 1950's a large crowd gathered at Whitburn to see Len Shackelton the famous Sunderland footballer, who was a cricket professional for Wearmouth. He was loudly applauded to the wicket, particularly by the crowd of youngsters there to see their football hero. Cries of "Shack! Shack! Good old Shack!" filled the air. Richard Heron (later president of the Durham Senior League) was fielding in the slips and heard Shack being greeted by wicket keeper Ron Emmerson after his tumultuous welcome by the large crowd. "By the way, what's your name young man? asks the wicket keeper. "Mine's Emmerson."

Ron Emmerson

Richard Heron

Len Shackelton

Mr Heron was responsible for the cutting down of the large sycamore tree in the ground. He arranged for a local firm of contractors to remove the tree at a nominal sum. He stated there were no tree preservation orders around in those days. It is said that lost cricket balls cascaded from the tree as it fell.

19

Above the infamous sycamore tree that was part of the village ground until the late forties early fifties, the tree was removed to allow batsmen to reach the boundaries without this major obstacle, numerous balls were recovered from the tree on its removal.

The outline marks the centre of the infamous sycamore tree.

Whitburn Cricket Club Third Team Champions 1954
R. Ward, A. Alder, N. Howe, R. Mcluskey, R. Paxton, N. Blyth, G. Cook, E. Smith, L. Sole,
J. Naisby, C. Bell.

The first womans' Cricket Team at Whitburn c1950
J. Farrow, A. Emmerson, J. Alder (A.P. Ashley's daughter), F. Percy, I. Stenton (nee Jones).
M. Heron, E. Mapstone, N. Brown, J. Bell (from S Reeders Book).

Whitburn Cricket Club First X1
Durham Senior League Champions 1964 and winners of the Sir Hedworth Williamson Cup
J.P.T. Bell, A. Coulthard, L. Gibbs, M. Allan, B. Turnbull, C. Bell, T. Young, T. Milton, E. Smith, W. Johnson,
D. Carr, K. Cooper, G. Crosby, N. Alder.

Contumacious Incident at Whitburn

In August 1963, the Sunderland Echo reported that Whitburn's picturesque ground had never seen the like. Their home match against Boldon ended when the home side walked off after they thought that Boldon's last man, skipper Don Hardy, had been caught, giving Whitburn a narrow victory. Hardy appeared to begin to walk off when he realised that umpire J.K.Bone had given him 'not out'. Despite the umpire's decision the Whitburn team departed to the pavilion leaving the umpire to draw the stumps and follow. The matter was passed to the Appeal Committee. At the ensuing inquiry Whitburn were alleged to be at fault in leaving the field before the completion of the match. Whitburn were fined five guineas. Mr. Tom Darling, League President stated, 'We were not concerned whether it was the right decision by the umpire. The important thing is that it is final. Whitburn should have remained on the field to finish the match.' As a result of this decision it is believed that the Whitburn captain that day, Barrie Connor never played cricket again. A sad result for a man described as a true gentleman.

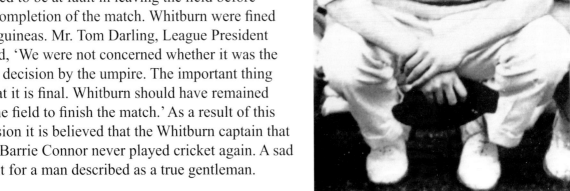

Barrie Connor Whitburn Club Captain 1957-1963.

Lance Gibbs

Lance Gibbs became the first professional in the Durham Senior League to earn £1,000.

Below are his statistics, during the 1964 championship winning season. Gibbs total number of wickets taken that season is still a Durham Senior League record.

Professional	Innings'	Runs	Average	Over's	Maidens	Runs	Wickets	Average
L.R. Gibbs	**20**	**169**	**10.6**	**552.1**	**171**	**1073**	**126**	**8.5**

Formal presentation at the Seaburn Hotel of the 1964 Durham Senior League Champions Cup
N. Alder, A. Alder, C. Bell, K. Cooper, M. Allan, B. Turnbull, J. Goodfellow, G. Crosby, Mrs. Evans,
E. Smith, Mr. Evans.

Five members of the successful 1964 Durham Senior League Championship Winning Side.
Back row: Dougie Bell, Brian Turnbull.
Front Row: Cliff Bell, Kenny Cooper, John Goodfellew.

A view of the new pavilion built in 1961 by LW Evans builder.
The club was officially opened on 26th April 1962, painted by Ron Thornton,
South Shields Cricket Club wicket keeper.

On May 22nd 1971 Alan Chapman, a local lad playing for Whitburn second X1 against South Shields second X1, achieved one of the greatest honours in the game of cricket. He took 10 wickets for 31 runs in an innings. This was only the third time this record had been achieved in the club's history.

N°	TIME IN OUT	BATSMAN	RUNS SCORED (Insert interim totals in heavy squares)	HOW OUT (Time each man for 50 and 100)	BOWLER	TOTAL
1		B MILLS	2 1 4 2 4 3 1 3 /	BOWLED	CHAPMAN	20
2		H KNIGHT	W. /	BOWLED	CHAPMAN	2
3		G McCORMACK	2 1 4 - 1 1 1 1 1 1 /	BOWLED	CHAPMAN	13
4		D FOSTER	2 /	ct EMMERSON	CHAPMAN	2
5		E GLEANY	/	ct EMMERSON	CHAPMAN	0
6		W GRAHAM	1 W 1 1 1 1 2 /	ct EMMERSON	CHAPMAN	9
7		A BARTHWICK	1 4 /	BOWLED	CHAPMAN	5
8		A WOODLAND	4 /	BOWLED	CHAPMAN	4
9		I BARTHWICK	2 /	c/o D ALLEN	CHAPMAN	2
10		M SEALES	/	L B W	CHAPMAN	0
11		S ALDER	1	NOT OUT		1

WHITBURN 2ND VERSUS SOUTH SHIELDS 2ND at SOUTH SHIELDS on 22ND MAY 1971
INNINGS OF SOUTH SHIELDS   TOSS WON BY WHITBURN
INNINGS COMMENCED 5.34   SUSPENDED FOR Rain Light Rule   INNINGS ENDED 7.19

EXTRAS:- BYES .... LEG BYES 1 1 1 1 1 1 .... WIDES .... NO BALLS 6

FALL OF WICKETS	1for 10	2for 31	3for 35	4for 35	5for 47	6for 52	7for 55	8for 55	9for 63	for 0 Wkts	TOTAL 64
TIME OF FALL OF EACH WKT	5.45	6.06	6.12	6.19	6.45	7.00	7.05	7.09	7.14	7.19	
BATSMEN IN PARTNERSHIP	1 and 2	1 and 3	3 and 4	3 and 5	3 and 6	3 and 7	3 and 8	8 and 9	9 and 10	10 and 11	

The other two players were W. Scott who took 10 for 14 at Seaham Harbour in a second X1 match against Seaham, on 9th August 1941, and Colin Sweeting who took 10 for 47 at Whitburn in a second X1 game against Burnmoor on 13th August 1951.

Colin Sweeting took 10-47 against Burnmoor.

Bill Scott took 10-14 against Seaham.

Alan Chapman with his grandfather's clock.

A young Alan Chapman.

Alan's grandfather C.J. 'Kit' Oates received a clock as a gift from Whitburn Cricket Club in 1933 for his services as Honorary Secretary to the club over a period of 13 years. Alan is still in possession of his grandfather's clock.

Whitburn Cricket Club First X1 1974

Durham Senior League Runners up, E.R. Armbrister Trophy Winners,
A.M.Brown Trophy Winners
D. Parnaby, C. Marshall, K.Waugh, A.A. Johnson, S.Betts,
A. Shields, M. Hunter, G.H. Crosby, W. Wimhurst,
E.W.Smith, W. Johnson, P.M. Freeman, A. Alder (Capt), W. Barker, B. Turnbull, W.H. Horsburgh.

Whitburn Cricket Club First X1 1977

Walter Shield, Tommy Wilkinson, Colin Marshall, Greg Hartson, Russ Muse, Alan Alder, Tony Shields,
Norman Shields, ?, Peter Freeman, Dave Parnaby, Barry Emmerson, Vic Hanson, Wilf Barker,
Barry Abe, Bill Horsburgh.

Six professionals have played for Whitburn Cricket Club
and also represented their countries at test cricket:

1950 Sid O'Linn (South Africa)

1963 Nasim-ul-Ghani (Pakistan)

1962, 1964, 1965 Lance Gibbs (West Indies)

1979 B.L. Cairns (New Zealand)

1981 Wasim Raja (Pakistan)

1995-96 Patterson Thompson (West Indies)

*Sid O'Linn
1950.*

*Lance Gibbs
1962, 64, 65.*

*Lance Cairns
1979.*

*Nasim Ul
Ghani 1963.*

*Patterson
Thompson
1995-96.*

*Wasim Raja
1981.*

Whitburn Second X1 pictured with the sponsors Bridge Street Motors Mitsubishi Colt before the league cup final at Whitburn.

A charity match for special needs children, between the 'Mini Birds' and Whitburn Cricketers on 10th September 1967.

WHITBURN CRICKET CLUB
CLUB PROFESSIONAL — STEVE GREENSWORD

COMMEMORATIVE MATCH
SUNDAY 29th AUGUST 1982

1964 LEAGUE CHAMPIONS		1982 TEAM SQUAD
K. COOPER *(Capt.)*		BILL HORSBURGH
A. ALDER		PETER FREEMAN
N. ALDER		WILF BARKER
M. R. ALLAN		TONY SHIELDS
C. C. P. BELL		RUSSELL MUSE
J. D. BELL		TOM WILKINSON
G. H. CROSBY	— V —	COLIN MARSHALL
F. D. CARR		GEORGE BROWN
T. W. MILTON		ALAN CHAPMAN
W. JOHNSON		RAY SOPPITT
B. M. TURNBULL		NORMAN SOPPITT
E. W. SMITH		BARRY EMMERSON
L. R. GIBBS *(Prof.)*		DAVID MOON
		DAVID NUNN
		STEVE GREENSWORD *(Prof.)*

ORIGINAL TEAM, NOT A MAN UNDER 40,
ALL HAVING UNDERGONE EXTENSIVE TRAINING
FOR THIS MATCH

FIT YOUNG MEN IN THEIR
PRIME SEASON OF SPORT

The above programme shows the teams who played a representative game on 29th August at the village ground. The programme described the **"original team as not having a man under forty all undergone extensive training for this match."** *The other team being* **"fit young men in their prime season of sport."**

Club Captain Wilf Barker 1975, 1981 and 1982.
He also represented Durham County Cricket Club
in 1970 whilst playing for Wearmouth.

29

The successful Whitburn junior's team pictured in 1987 with cricket legend Geoffrey Boycott during the TSB under 16 six-a-side competition at Headingley.
Official, Michael Smith, Geoffrey Boycott, Neil Ayre, Anthony Jude, Paul Cook, Official, Scott Davis, David Abdy, Paul Ord, Mark Hazard.

The Whitburn Cricket Club Juniors won the August 1987 Gun and Moore Youth Merit Award in 1987 in association with the magazine cricket world.

Whitburn under 15 squad and supporters on tour in 1988. They played matches in Halesowen, Stourbridge and Worcestershire.

Whitburn staged two very entertaining matches at the village ground over the weekend of 23rd/24th September 1989. A representative Durham Select X1 played the first class county cricket sides Leicestershire and Middlesex. In those sides were England test captains David Gower and Mike Gatting.

Mike Gatting

David Gower

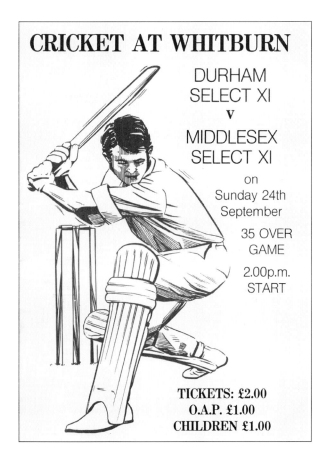

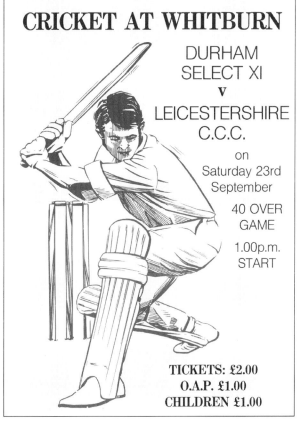

Copies of the two programmes used during the weekend 23rd/24th September 1989.

The cricket ground came under the ownership of several business men. Initially, Mr Laurie Evans, who bought Whitburn Hall and the cricket club grounds in 1961, built a new club and changing rooms. This was officially opened in May of 1962 by Mr and Mrs Evans.

However, in the late part of the 1980s Mr Evans put the club up for sale for a 'Hope Value' which means an elevated market value, reflecting the prospect of some more valuable use or development in excess of the existing use. This could include building on the land. The thought of the sale of the club and ground caused a lot of anger and frustration that cricket would be lost to the village. Around this time there was comment that the local authority may place a compulsory purchase order on the club house and land.

In the meantime, Mr. Alan Burridge purchased the property from Evans Builders for a sum of about £75,000. Then two local businessmen, Mr Mattie Roseberry and Mr. Barry Emmerson, purchased the

New metal entrance gates.

club. The latter had played cricket at the club since his childhood. He made some distinctive club house alterations, re-carpeting and redecorating the first floor bar area and replacing the old entrance gates with a new metal variety.

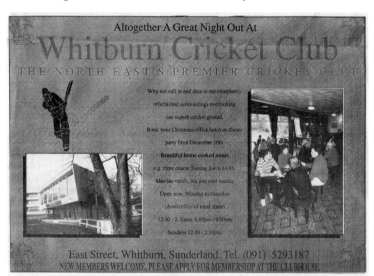

Club advert in the Sunderland Echo November 1990.

The two men attempted to resurrect Whitburn Cricket club's fortunes. Unfortunately, in 1990 after Mr Emmerson's business enterprise at the club started to wane, the clubhouse was closed in respect of social activity, now club quiz nights and other meetings were held in the local 'Jolly Sailor' public house.

In 1991 the club members took over the running of the club and eventually purchased the club from Mr Emmerson for the sum of £125,000 pounds. This was thanks to two grants, one from the National Lottery and the other from the Sports Council Foundation for Sports and Arts, amounting to the sum of £108,000.

The remaining sum of £17,000 came from a local brewery as a loan. This loan was eventually repaid and in 1996 the cricket club could announce ***"the return of the club back to the members."***

Whitburn Cricket Club 1990 Saunders cup winning team
M. Bell, N. Ayre, M. Shotton, R. Muse, M. Smith, A. Shields, R. Romero, A. Wilkinson
G. Ventress, D. Bell (Capt), S. Old, S. Emmerson.

Ex senior league umpire Wally Nunn on
the gate in July 1991.

Peter Elliott painting the scoreboard.

Sunderland footballers who played cricket for Whitburn Leighton James, Derek Forster Dennis Tueart, and Richie Pitt.

Whitburn First X1 1994

P. Cook, D. Borthwick, S. Robinson, R. Muse, N. Ayre, D. Abdy,
I. Renton, M. Sygrove, G. Borthwick (Capt), B. Hart, S. Emmerson.

Whitburn Cricket Club 2005
Winners of the Armourpost Security Shutters DRV Challenge Cup
M. Smith, N. Johnson, E. Elstob, I. Elliott, A. Turns, C. Henderson (Scorer),
P. Cook, N. Ayre, P. Shields, D. Bell (Capt), A. Thorpe, J. Dunn, G.V. Ventress.

Some of the junior members involved in the 'Nat West- ECB Cricket Force' day 2011.

Whitburn Cricket Club
Durham Senior League T20 Champions 2011
A. Chambers, A. Turns, A. Bannister, L. Henderson, N. Johnson, I. Elliott, R. Carty, N. Ayre,
C. Smith, P. Shields, D. Bell (Capt), P. Marshall, S. Walker (Pro).

Whitburn Cricket Club Pavilion 2011.

Groundsmans store/old tea hut.

Cliff Bell recalls that after the war players would leave the ground to go up East Street to the 'Smith and Stephenson' cafe for teas until a marquee was erected in the ground around about 1948. Subsequently, the above tea hut was built by players, club officials and local craftsmen and is now used as the grounds man's store.

The famous and well known 'Tea ladies' sitting outside the pavilion with Barry Emmerson in 1994. L to R Mrs Chapman, Mrs Hetherington, Barry Emmerson, Mrs Merriman and Mrs Emmerson.

A list of Whitburn Cricket Club first team successes over the past 150 years

1ˢᵗ X1 Durham County League

League Champions	1896, 1898

1st X1 Durham Senior League Record

League Champions	1923, 1924, 1925, 1926, 1932, 1950, 1964
Saunders Cup	1921, 1923, 1956, 1990
Sir Hedworth Williamson Cup	1956, 1957, 1960, 1961, 1962, 1963, 1964, 1965
Elizabeth Robson Cup	1962
E.R. Armbrister Trophy	1974, 1975
A.M. Brown Trophy	1974
J.W. Wood Cup	1984
Grangetown Florists Bowl	1976, 1977, 1981, 1985
Smith Print Trophy	1977
GA Property Services Cup	1989
Durham County League Championship	1896, 1898
Armourpost Security Shutters DRV Challenge Cup	2005
Durham Cricket Board 6 a side Championship	2006
Captain Ramsden Shield	2006
Regency Windows Trophy	2007
Durham Senior League Twenty 20 Cup	2011

Whitburn celebrate a wicket in a match against Sunderland at Ashbrooke during the 1980's.

Whitburn Players who have represented
Durham County Cricket Club from 1882-1992 whilst playing for Whitburn:

A.P. Ashley	1920-1924
J.P.T. Bell	1920
K.D. Biddulph	1969
B.L. Cairns	1979
C.L. Dobson	1897-1901
F. Dobson	1888
T.K. Dobson (Snr)	1886-1896
T.K. Dobson (Jnr)	1922-1936
W.A. Dobson	1919-1925
W.S. Dobson	1898-1905
P.M. Freeman	1967-1971
S. Greensword	1982-1983
C.W.H. Hawley	1890
A.A. Johnson	1973
J. Kelsall	1926
J.R. Milne	1933
W. Scott	1941-44
J.W. Smith	1924-25
T.G. Smith	1925
R.I. Smyth	1974
Wasim Raja	1981
F.C. Williamson	1899
R.E. Wylde	1939

Len Ashurst.

Former Sunderland football stalwart Len Ashurst is currently raising funds to upgrade facilities at Whitburn Cricket Club, including new seating and an electronic scoreboard.

Len, a former Whitburn cricketer, is pictured above on the first of the new wooden seating in front of the old grade two listed balustrade which separated the ground from the old Whitburn Hall.

Former foreign secretary and local Member of Parliament David Miliband seen here in 2012 with former Sunderland footballing 'great' Len Ashurst planning another of Len's fund raising events for the club.

Relaying the artificial wicket at Whitburn Cricket Club in 2012 by the sports surface specialist Pinnacle.

Players from days gone by would not recognise the equipment available today. Here players Andy Turns and Neil Ayre are practicing in the nets with the new electronic bowling machine which can fire a ball at 99 miles per hour.

Captains 1952-2012

1952	R.H. Percy	1973	A. Alder	1994	G. Borthwick
1953	A. Alder snr	1974	A. Alder	1995	G. Borthwick
1954	J.B. Bell	1975	W. Barker	1996	G. Borthwick
1955	J.B. Bell	1976	V. Hanson	1997	N. Ayre/A. Shields
1956	R.H. Percy	1977	V.Hanson	1998	A. Shields
1957	B.P. Connor	1978	P.M. Freeman	1999	P. Shields
1958	B.P. Connor	1979	P.M. Freeman	2000	P. Shields
1959	B.P. Connor	1980	W. Barker	2001	K. Burdett
1960	B.P. Connor	1981	W. Barker	2002	K. Burdett
1961	B.P. Connor	1982	S. Greensword	2003	A. Shields
1962	B.P. Connor	1983	S. Greensword	2004	D. Bell
1963	B.P. Connor	1984	R.A. Muse	2005	D. Bell
1964	K. Cooper	1985	R.A. Muse	2006	D. Bell
1965	K. Cooper	1986	R.A. Muse	2007	D. Bell
1966	F.D. Carr	1987	W. Barker	2008	D. Bell
1967	C.C.P. Bell	1988	W. Barker	2009	D. Bell
1968	C.C.P. Bell	1989	D. Bell	2010	D. Bell
1969	C.C.P. Bell	1990	D. Bell	2011	D. Bell
1970	M.R. Allen	1991	D. Bell	2012	D. Bell
1971	P.M. Freeman	1992	D. Culling		
1972	A. Alder	1993	D. Culling		

Ex captains Steven Greensword and Tony Shields.

David Bell the club's longest serving Captain.

Professionals 1952-2012

1952	R.O. Lowerson	1973	A.A. Johnson	1994	
1953	R.O. Lowerson	1974	A.A. Johnson	1995	P.I.C. Thompson
1954	R.O. Lowerson	1975	A.A. Johnson	1996	P.I.C. Thompson
1955	F.C. Lucas	1976	B. Islam	1997	A. Wilson
1956	N.G. Lorraine	1977	G. Hartshorne	1998	S. Mascarenhas
1957	N.G. Lorraine	1978	J.S. Coyle	1999	K. Burdett
1958	N.G. Lorraine	1979	B.L. Cairns	2000	K. Burdett
1959		1980	R. Soppit	2001	K. Burdett
1960		1981	W.H. Raja	2002	K. Burdett
1961		1982	S. Greensword	2003	
1962	L.R. Gibbs	1983	S. Greenswor	2004	A. Thorpe
1963		1984	C.C. Alleyne	2005	A. Thorpe
1964	L.R. Gibbs	1985	C.C. Alleyne	2006	A. Thorpe
1965	L.R. Gibbs	1986	C.C. Alleyne	2007	A. Thorpe
1966		1987	S. Greensword	2008	L. Cullen
1967	D. Ferguson	1988	S. Greensword	2009	C. Wood
1968	D. Ferguson	1989	C.A. Davidson	2010	S. Walker
1969	K. Biddulh	1990	J.S. Sykes	2011	S. Walker
1970	K. Biddulh	1991		2012	S. Walker
1971	K. Biddulh	1992	A.S. Patel		
1972	A.A. Johnson	1993	A.S. Patel		

Whitburn is a very progressive club which has moved with the times. It has a very strong youth policy which includes female players and there are under 11, 13, 15 and 18 youth teams which underpin robust adult First, Second and Third teams. The generous community spirit of the club and its supporters has manifested itself in this history. It is thanks to everyone who has produced documents and photographs from cupboards, attics and sheds that I have been able to add to my personal research and been able to piece together a history which I hope is truly worthy of this excellent club.

Whitburn Cricket Club is celebrating the sesquicentennial anniversary of 150 years of formalised cricket in the village. The book has touched on some but not all of the players who have graced this picturesque village ground; my apologies to those I have omitted. I believe that the place cricket has played in the lives of generations of Whitburn people was best described in 1949 by Sunderland Echo correspondent Jack Wood. He wrote, "There is local pride too, in the cricket ground, a pride of which the visitor is conscious the moment he steps into the shadow of historic Whitburn Hall, you don't watch cricket at Whitburn Hall.... you live the game, and feel deeply conscious of that past which began almost a hundred years ago."
Bon Voyage Whitburn, enjoy your journey through the next 150 years.

Chairman, player and ex captain Russell Muse
now taking the club into the new millennium.

Acknowledgements

I wish to thank the following people who have kindly helped me in this book:
Alan Alder; Bobby Ayre; Cliff Bell; Dave Bell; Alan Brett; Andrew Clark;
Phil Curtis; Ian Elliott; Barry Emmerson; Brian Hastings; Richard Heron; Sasha Hill;
William Horsburgh; Brian Hunt; Norman Kirtlan; Dave Larkin; Alan Lock; Russell Muse;
George Nairn; Sybil Reeder;
Alan Simpson; Eric Smith and Marge Smith: Mary Stephenson;
Sarah Stoner (Sunderland Echo); Frank Turns; Sunderland Antiquarians Society;
Sunderland Library; South Shields Library; Whitburn Cricket Club Officials and members;
Michael Wake & Steve Olley, CVN Print.

References

100 years of Durham County Cricket Club by Brian Hunt
Sunderland Echo articles by CA Smith
Memories of Whitburn by Sybil Reeder
Articles by Mary Stephenson
History of Durham Senior League by Ray Palliser

Finally, my dear wife and mentor Stephanie Yearnshire MBE, for her clarity of thought,
vision and understanding during my research and during the time I was attached to the computer
for days on end.

ISBN: 978-1-906721-50-3

Printed by CVN Print, Maxwell Street, South Shields, Tyne & Wear, NE33 4PU. Tel: 0191 455 3703 www.cvnprint.com